We the People

Arthur St. Clair and the Northwest Ordinance

Editorial Director, Joseph S. McNamara

THE HILLSDALE COLLEGE AMERICAN HERITAGE SERIES

ARTHUR ST. CLAIR

From an oil painting by Peale, now in Independence Hall, Philadelphia.
Reprinted with permission of Joyce Office Products.

I. "An Indian Country at War"

On Tuesday, July 15, 1788, Governor Arthur St. Clair addressed the citizens of Marietta, on the north bank of the Ohio River, and he read to the assembled citizens "An Ordinance for the government of the territory of the United States northwest of the river Ohio." The *Northwest Ordinance* quickly achieved the force of constitutional law. Wherever Americans pushed into new frontiers for the next hundred years, they made governments and became states according to the rules outlined in this remarkable document.

St. Clair hoped to find joy in "reducing [the] country from a state of nature to a state of civilization." His mind could see "vast forests converted into arable fields, and cities rising in places which were lately the habitations of wild beasts"; it gave him "a pleasure something like that attendant upon creation." He could even imagine being a party to God's Providence, "when all the nations of the earth shall become the kingdom of Jesus Christ."

But he also warned the pioneers of Marietta, "You have upon your frontiers numbers of savages, and, too often, hostile nations." These were the fundamental facts they had to face. British Canada lay not far to the north. Spaniards wary of American expansion waited at the Mississippi, on the western edge of the territory. The British still occupied forts in American territory (at Detroit, for example), despite the War for Independence being five years in the past.

Most important, and most dangerous, the strongest Indian nations in the territory recognized no right of American settlement anywhere north of the Ohio River!

Governor St. Clair counseled "a good understanding with the natives." "Treat them on all occasions with kindness," he said, "and with the strictest regard for justice." But St. Clair knew in his heart that the Miamis and their great war chief, Little Turtle, were in no mood to receive kindness. He knew that representatives of the Six Nations, the great Iroquois people, were in Ohio seeking a confederation of all the western Indians. He knew that the Shawnees, Potawatomis, Chippewas, and dozens of other tribes would slaughter Americans who tried to settle without their permission in the lands covered by the Northwest Ordinance. And he knew the British would help the Indians.

In fact, for seven years the settlements in the Old Northwest would be in a state of what amounted to permanent siege warfare. St. Clair was under orders to obtain whatever treaties he could, with any tribe that would listen. His instructions from Congress read, "Every exertion must be made to defeat all confederations and combinations among the tribes." Later this method turned into a policy: entreat with tribes singly, or in small groups, and get them to sell their lands; divide them, in order to prevent them from forming great confederacies. Keeping Indians divided, which is how they existed in their natural groupings, treating them as a series of separate nations, would buy the Americans time, until the new frontier settlements were able

Northwest Territory

to deal with the Indians from a position of strength.

But in 1788 the task was to survive. The very first law adopted in the Northwest Territory was for the formation and maintenance of a militia. There were fewer than 600 regular army troops in the entire territory by early 1789. The need for a treaty was great. This situation produced one of those colorful and curious incidents that tell us much about the nature of frontier life.

In November of 1788 two Mohawks came to Fort Harmar (at Marietta), representing the great chief of the Longhouse (the Six Nations of the Iroquois confederacy), Joseph Brant. Brant's influence was great all over the Indian world, although he had just weeks before failed to bring unity to the western tribes. One of the messengers was Brant's son, Isaac, who apparently made a good impression at Fort Harmar. Their news for the governor: Joseph Brant wants peace, but he also wants St. Clair to meet him at the falls of the Muskingum River, some fifty miles from Marietta, rather than at the white man's fort. Suspecting a trick, and knowing more than Brant thought he knew about the quarrels among the Indians, St. Clair sent them back with word that he would soon reply by his own messenger.

Hamilton "Ham" Kerr was sent with St. Clair's refusal, a reply Joseph Brant would certainly not want to hear. Kerr's errand, then, was very dangerous. A day out from the fort, Kerr saw tracks. Keeping the river in sight he crept up on a bluff and raised up to look around. Hearing a woman's

Joseph Brant, Mohawk chief. Engraving by J. R. Smith after a painting by G. Romney. (The New York Public Library.)

laugh, he came down toward the river and ran into Louisa St. Clair, the governor's sixteen-year-old daughter! She was on horseback, dressed like an Indian, with a short rifle slung across her body.

Ham Kerr was so stupefied he lost his speech. Anyone who knew the beautiful Louisa shouldn't have been too astonished to see her there: she was headstrong, determined, an excellent tracker and marksman, more at home than most men on a horse or a pair of ice skates. One of her relatives said she could rival Diana as a huntress, if she used a bow instead of her rifle. She told Ham Kerr that she was determined to meet the great Mohawk chief, and to carry her father's letter to him.

Ham tried to turn her back; she laughed and mocked his forest clothes, which included an Indian breechcloth and kerchiefed hair. The young ranger fed her some dried deer meat and guarded her through the night, then obediently hid while she dashed off through the woods with the letter and was soon captured by Brant's Mohawks. Chief Joseph (Thayendanegea, "Burning Stick"), despite his very real savagery as an accomplished Iroquois warrior, was also a Christian, an English-educated gentleman, and a scholar who had translated the Episcopal *Book of Common Prayer* into the language of the Six Nations. He would not consider harming the daughter of Governor St. Clair. But neither would he be a party to the governor's treaty.

Isaac Brant insisted upon returning with Louisa to Fort Harmar, as he said, to guard the warrior who was assigned to guard her. Completely captivated by this brave and beautiful woman, he asked Arthur St. Clair for his daughter in marriage! She apparently favored the proposal. The governor couldn't bear to give his favorite child to an Indian, and refused.

The story may not be factual in all its particulars. Brant's biographer calls it a "fanciful" legend, in part because it can't be shown that Louisa was with her father in the territory that early, in part because it seems to go against the grain of Isaac Brant's character (he is said to have greatly disliked whites), and in part because there is no mention of it in Arthur St. Clair's papers. But nobody doubts that it was consistent with Louisa's daring frontier character, and we know that the setting and dates are accurate. It was also a persistent legend in the St. Clair family, and it tells us much about the very complicated relations among real whites and real Indians, as opposed to the stereotypes often promoted by changing cultural fashions.

This sad little tale in the midst of the much larger tragedy of Indian-white warfare probably didn't affect the course of events. A treaty was signed on January 11, 1789, and it gave the settlers the right to most of Ohio. But the most powerful tribes were not parties to it. Little Turtle of the Miamis remained fiercely opposed, and in 1790 soundly defeated a 1400-man army sent out to clear the Maumee River valley of Indian opposition.

In October of 1791 St. Clair himself took the field in command of an army of almost 2000 men, over 1400 of them militia. General St. Clair had been a competent officer in the

War for Independence, but knew little about Indian warfare. The militiamen were pitiful soldiers, recruited "from prisons, wheelbarrows and brothels at two dollars a month." By November 3, after Little Turtle had drawn them into the upper Wabash River area, St. Clair had to have his regulars guard the supply train from his other men, and over 600 had deserted. And although the governor had chosen good high ground to defend, it was in terrain that the Indians liked–covered with trees. Little Turtle attacked in the early morning, his warriors crawling low and firing out of the brush. The Kentucky militia broke and ran immediately. Artillerymen stood their ground, but filled the air with smoke, and the Indians picked off soldiers individually, causing great panic.

Fort Washington, established in 1789. From this fort Governor St. Clair started northward in 1791 to chastise the Indians. His army was completely defeated by Little Turtle.

St. Clair rallied his regulars for a bayonet attack, and the battle raged for most of the day. Indians fired effectively from the trees and attacked almost at will in sporadic but vicious hand-to-hand fighting. There was no question of St. Clair's courage. Despite great pain from gout, he rode back and forth encouraging his men and leading several countercharges. He never left the front line until, hopelessly surrounded in the late afternoon, with more than half his army down, he ordered a retreat. They fought through their encirclement, abandoned most of their equipment ("not a horse was left alive to have it drawn off"), and fought and ran more than thirty miles to relative safety. Only 580 men returned home. The wounded, left behind, were tortured and slaughtered.

General St. Clair had four horses shot from under him during the battle. Eight bullets pierced his clothes and hat. One grazed his cheek and took off a lock of his gray hair. Isaac Brant led some Chippewas during the fight. It is said that he ordered the Indians not to kill the white chief.

After this defeat, St. Clair gave up the military side of his duties and went back to being a fulltime governor. President Washington and his Secretary of War, Henry Knox, decided that the time had come for a systematic campaign against Little Turtle. This was not, in the minds of the Americans, simply an aggres-

Fort St. Clair (near Eaton, Ohio). Built in the winter of 1791-2. (Courtesy of Mrs. Mary Gould Brooke.) Reprinted with permission of Joyce Office Products.

sive campaign for Indian lands. The Miamis and Six Nations (and many other tribes) had been formal allies of the British during the War for Independence and as such had to be considered defeated nations. That the British were still giving aid and comfort to Indians, and doing so from forts on American soil, meant in effect that the War for Independence had not yet ended in the West. St. Clair had pointed this out to various Indian leaders. Some accepted the idea; some rejected it. But the administration of George Washington decided, after St. Clair's disastrous defeat, to act on the principle.

General Anthony Wayne, a meticulous planner and stern

disciplinarian, was chosen for the task. He spent almost three years training an army, building up the forts St. Clair had started, and learning from earlier American mistakes. During that time almost five-sixths of the general expenses of the national government were directed to the war in the West. "Mad Anthony" built well. In August, 1794, he crushed a less competent successor to Little Turtle, and the demoralized Indians signed the Treaty of Greenville in 1795. They gave up most of Ohio and the lands around Detroit, Chicago, and Vincennes. On a different front, Jay's Treaty was signed in the same year. The British agreed to evacuate all forts in the Northwest Territory. The War for Independence was finally over.

II. St. Clair: Developer-Pioneer and Nationalist

The main effect of the treaty of 1795 was to open the gates that had held back the movement of people to the frontier. In 1795 the entire population of the Northwest Territory was just

a few thousand, not even enough to qualify for a territorial legislature under the terms of the Northwest Ordinance. By the time St. Clair left the territory in 1803, Ohio was ready to become a state, and tens of thousands of settlers had emigrated to the Ohio, Muskingum, Scioto, and Miami river valleys. Many more were pouring into the Western Re-

serve, up on the shores of Lake Erie. While the immediate and early task of the governor had been to hold off the Indians, his greater job was to lay the groundwork for civil government. For this work Arthur St. Clair was well prepared.

He was a Scotsman by birth (March 23, 1736). He came to the American colonies in 1757 as a British soldier, to fight in the French and Indian War. St. Clair never went home. Entitled by birth and education to be an officer, he associated with colonial gentlemen. He married Phoebe Bayard in Boston in 1760. She was a niece, on her mother's side, of Massachusetts Governor James Bowdoin, and she brought to the marriage a legacy of 14,000 pounds sterling. This made young St. Clair wealthy by the standards of the day, capable of living a life of ease.

Instead he moved his family to the Pennsylvania frontier. By purchase and by land grant (for his service in the war) St. Clair put together a large estate in the Ligonier Valley, near Pittsburgh. He probably owned about 16,000 acres of land by the mid-1780s. As the largest landholder on the Pennsylvania frontier, St. Clair spent much of his time in public service, much like the country squires of the old country or of rural Virginia and Maryland. By 1771 he had served as surveyor, judge, and member of the Governor's Council for the Cumberland District. In the next few years he also helped in the founding of Westmoreland County (and held several important county offices), contended against Virginia claims in Pennsylvania country, and conducted negotiations with Indians who, as usual, resented encroaching civilization. Much of what he would later be asked to do in the Northwest Territory he did on a smaller scale in his own neighborhood. Arthur and Phoebe St. Clair also raised seven children. The daring Louisa was born in Ligonier.

"The Hermitage," Chestnut Ridge, Pennsylvania. (Restored by Wm. G. Ward, architect, from an illustration in American Monthly Magazine, Vol. XXI.) Reprinted with permission of Joyce Office Products.

Arthur St. Clair was not a buckskin-pioneer. He was a developer-pioneer. People who knew him said he was tall (which could mean anything over five feet, eight inches in those days), always carefully dressed, and had a light complexion, remarkable grey-blue eyes, and chestnut hair. His portrait, done in his early middle age by Charles Willson Peale, shows a handsome and robust soldier, giving forth an air of authority and slight impatience. He helped to recruit families to the frontier, many of them Scots and Scots-Irish, who always proved to be good (if somewhat unruly) frontiersmen. He established law and order, and served the government.

In 1775 St. Clair became a member of the Committee of Public Safety of Westmoreland County. This was a patriot organization, charged mainly in that year with organizing citizens to defend their rights as British subjects. Later it became the unofficial local government during the War for Independence. It isn't clear what prompted St. Clair to declare for the American cause, but he wrote many of the liberty-loving resolutions passed by western Pennsylvanians in 1775. When a delegation led by fellow Scot James Wilson came west to support fellow patriots, St. Clair accompanied them to discuss neutrality with neighboring Indians. He came up with a plan to raise a small army and march against the British at Detroit. Although it was not approved by the Continental Congress (George Rogers Clark later gained great fame for conceiving a similar plan), St. Clair took his force of 400 Pennsylvanians up to Canada. Thus began his second military career.

He fought in upper New York, at Trenton and Princeton, at Brandywine, with Nathaniel Greene in the south, and at Yorktown. He became a valued friend to Washington and to Henry Knox, and he admired the young Alexander Hamilton. He gave brave service and became a general. Unfortunately, he also was known as the officer who had to surrender the American fort at Ticonderoga, an action for which a court-martial completely exonerated him.

After the war he went home to Ligonier and prospered. Mrs. St. Clair, although enjoying good physical health through a long life, broke under the strain of hard frontier life and her crushing responsibilities during Arthur's many years of absence. Even comparative wealth couldn't insulate frontier women from the strain of physical labor and isolation. She became a mental invalid, cared for at home by her children.

St. Clair was gone during much of the 1780s as well. Convinced that the Pennsylvania constitution was dangerously democratic and unstable because of its unicameral legislature, he worked to have it replaced. In 1785 the citizens of the state elected him to the national Congress. This was under the Articles of Confederation government, before the adoption of the Constitution of 1787. He became President of the Congress, in effect the highest office in the land, and was presiding over it when the Northwest Ordinance was passed on July 13, 1787.

He didn't seek the post of governor of the new territory. He already had great power and a lucrative office. His congressional and Pennsylvania friends virtually forced him to take the job, thinking it would provide well for his large family and give him a chance to be with them more often. St. Clair later called his acceptance "the most imprudent act" of his life, but he also had the "laudable ambition of becoming the father of a country, and laying the foundation for the happiness of millions yet unborn." Who could resist, in this new country, participating in an "act of creation?"

III. An American Myth:
Free Men in the Wilderness

So the developer-pioneer went off to Marietta, Ohio, into the cauldron of "an Indian country at war." During those years of war, it was also St. Clair's responsibility to erect the framework of civil government on the foundation of the Northwest Ordinance. Laws, courts, and local governments would be his chief concerns. He wasn't surprised to find that they were easier to consider than to construct.

Victor Collot, *Voyage dans l'Amerique.* Atlas. 1826 - Marietta, Ohio, about 1800. Reprinted with permission.

To consider properly the task St. Clair faced, let us turn to one of the most enduring of American myths: the "free man in the wilderness." We use "myth" in this case, not in the contemporary meaning of something contrary to fact, but in the ancient meaning of heroic stories which help us to explain eternal truths about ourselves as a people. Myths tell us about our origins, what is truly important to us; they also teach us what behavior brings honor and shame. They are thus "truer" than mere factual accounts, because they represent the moral imagination, the highest principles of our culture.

During Arthur St. Clair's lifetime, the legend of Daniel Boone raised his frontier exploits almost to the level of myth. In 1823, the mythical character of the free man in the wilderness leaped off the pages of the novel *The Pioneers*, written by

James Fenimore Cooper. The free man was a buckskin-pioneer named Natty Bumppo. Americans recognized him immediately, and Cooper unfolded him variously as Hawkeye, the Pathfinder, the Deerslayer, and Leatherstocking in a total of five novels. He is perhaps America's *unique* mythic hero.

Cooper introduces us to Natty as an old man, nearly at his "three-score years and ten." But Natty is still quite a man, living in a remote cabin in the woods of central New York, in the hills where the Delaware and Susquehanna rivers rise. This was once the easternmost territory of the Iroquois, closed to white settlement until after the War for Independence (which Natty tells us he fought in), opened up by developer-pioneers only in the 1790s.

Natty has no need for law; he disciplines himself to live in harmony with nature, accepting its challenges and living off its bounty. There is no greater hunter. At age sixty-eight, Natty outshoots everyone around, knocking the head off a turkey at seventy-five paces on his first shot. While others net fish out of beautiful Otsego Lake, Natty uses a spear and gets just the right trout. He hits a dove on the fly and a panther ("painter") at an impossible angle as the animal is about to devour a beautiful young woman. Life was dangerous, but Natty can say with a later hero: "I never killed a man that didn't need killing; I never shot an animal except for meat."

He's unchurched, but noble, and unlettered: "I am a plain, unlarned man that has sarved both the king and his country, in his day, ag'in the French and savages, but never so much as looked into a book, or larnt a letter of scholarship, in my born days. I've never seen the use of such indoor work." He has no family, except the friends to whom he is unfailingly loyal. He moves his cabin when its front door gets more than a few feet from an ample supply of firewood.

Natty's life is simple, and he has no need for any of the institutions of society. But the problem of *The Pioneers* is, Natty's beloved woods stand on the precipice of civilization.

The action of the novel pits the buckskin-pioneer against the developer-pioneer. Marmaduke Temple has acquired Natty's woods and has come to build a society: "To his eye, where others saw nothing but a wilderness, towns, manufactories, bridges, canals, mines, and all the other resources of an old country were constantly presenting themselves." Judge Temple is a fictional portrait of James Fenimore Cooper's own father, who built Cooperstown, New York; the novelist lived what he wrote. Marmaduke brings in an Episcopal minister; he starts an academy for young scholars; he recruits storekeepers, farmers, and tradesmen.

Natty goes for none of it. "Heigh-ho!" he says, "I never know'd preaching come into a settlement but it made game scarce, and raised the price of gunpowder." He doesn't like the farmers, either: "No, no, Judge. It's the farmers that makes the game scarce, and not the hunters." Most of all, Natty reserves his contempt for the laws Marmaduke introduces, especially the game laws. "But it was a comfortable hunting ground then," he tells a young friend, "and would have been so to this day, but for the money of Marmaduke Temple, and *the twisty ways of the law.*"

Although it becomes clear that both are honorable men, one wants order and civilization; the other wants freedom and nature. They clash over the game laws: Natty kills a buck out of season, and then resists arrest. A posse finally brings the old man in, and he is tried under the forms of the Common Law, scrupulously fairly, with Marmaduke presiding as judge.

This part of the action is enlivened by the fact that, just days before the trial, Natty had saved the judge's only daughter from being mauled by a "painter" in the forest. Her heart, and the hearts of most of the villagers, are on Natty's side. And the old hunter is not above playing tunes of sympathy on their heartstrings. Marmaduke stands firm: "Would any society be tolerable...where the ministers of justice are to be opposed by men armed with rifles? Is it for this that I have tamed the wilderness?"

The jury convicts Natty. His sentence involves a month's imprisonment, among other things, and a remarkable exchange occurs. Natty wails over "the wickedness of shutting up an old man that has spent his days, as one may say, where he could always look into the windows of heaven." Marmaduke protests, "I must be governed by the law —" And Natty breaks in, "Talk to me not of law, Marmaduke Temple. Did the beast of the forest mind your laws when it was thirsty and hungering after the blood of your own child! She was kneeling to her God for a greater favor than I ask, and he heard her; and if you now say no to my prayers, do you think he will be deaf?" Natty pulls out all the emotional stops: "I've traveled these mountains when you was no judge, but an infant in your mother's arms; and I feel as if I had a right and a privilege to travel them ag'in afore I die."

This free man caged! Emotion, the heart, loyalty, natural right seem to line up on Natty's side. Later, talking with his daughter, Bess, who takes the hunter's part, Judge Temple insists that "the sanctity of the laws must be respected." Against her emotional defense of the old man, Marmaduke states flatly that "society cannot exist without wholesome restraints." While he gives her money to pay Natty's fine, Marmaduke gets to the core of his belief: "but try to remember, Elizabeth, *that the laws alone remove us from the condition of the savages*; that he has been criminal, and that his judge was thy father."

This, then, is what is between the hunter and the judge. Heart and head, nature and society, yes; but the bedrock issue is not simply a matter of the law. Man in nature, man in society: what lies behind their conflict is a conviction about human nature. Natty believes that there is simple decency in the human heart, and that it needs to be released from the constraints of civilization. He knows that the free man can discipline himself to the rhythms of nature and live in accordance with nature's laws. He may be uncouth, but never savage. The beast is in the forest, and the free man can cope with him. Marmaduke knows just as deeply that the real beast is not in the forest, but in the human heart itself. Only the duties of community life, the bonds of family, church, and town can keep it restrained.

Natty's myth, the myth of the free man in the wilderness, was and is uniquely powerful and appealing in American culture. Like Marmaduke Temple, Arthur St. Clair never believed it. But he had to face it head on in the Northwest Territory, if he was to carry off his "act of creation."

IV. "A Good Government, Well Administered"

Adam, as the first man, got to name all the creatures of the earth and the sea and air. St. Clair, as the first governor, got to name many places in the new territory. The first four counties he formed were named Washington, Hamilton, Knox, and St. Clair. Names tell us much about a person's loyalties, and about his beliefs.

St. Clair Home, 8th Street, near Main, Cincinnati. (Restored by William G. Ward, architect.) Reprinted with permission of Joyce Office Products.

St. Clair went down the Ohio River in early 1789, to the little town with the whimsical name of Losantiville. Now and then such a name turns up in that area, a legacy of Thomas Jefferson's earlier proposals: Polypotamia, Assenisipia, Pelisipia, and the like. The Governor promptly changed Losantiville to Cincinnati, and it became his capitol.

Cincinnati was named for the Society of the Cincinnati, an organization formed in 1783 of officers of the Continental Line. It was after Cincinnatus, who in Roman tradition left his fields, assumed the powers of a dictator, went out and saved Rome from its enemies, then gave up all his powers and returned to the plow. The republican patriot-farmer-soldier was the ideal of Washington's army. The Society sought to keep alive the ideals of liberty for which they had fought, to honor their French brothers who had fought with them, and to aid widows and orphans of deceased members. More important, it was a fraternal society of nationalists, men with "an unalterable determination to promote and cherish between the respective states, that union and National honor" they felt was crucial to the future. Washington was to be its president for life. Alexander Hamilton, Henry Knox, and Arthur St. Clair were founding members.

St. Clair brought to the territory a national vision of government and a tremendous loyalty to his President and to the first Secretaries of War and the Treasury. He was convinced that a "good government, well administered, is the first of blessings to a people." He also brought strong powers under the Northwest Ordinance, which would allow a determined governor to exercise a kind of institutional immortality.

The Congress decreed that the Ordinance of 1787 had constitutional force in all the territory bounded by the Ohio River on the south, the Great Lakes on the north, the Mississippi River on the west, and Pennsylvania on the east. Its articles were to be considered "as articles of compact, between the original States and the people and States in the said territory, and forever remain unalterable." It was meant to create a temporary government for colonial lands and a process through which territories could become states equal in every respect to the original states of the Union.

The Governor's powers during the transition were enormous. He was almost a monarch, although of course he was responsible to the Congress of the United States. He had full legislative power (along with three judges appointed by Congress) and the power to administer the laws; he was commander in chief of all militia; he had full appointive power over all civil officials; and he could divide up the territory into counties, townships, and court jurisdictions as he saw fit. We have already seen that he had the power to name places.

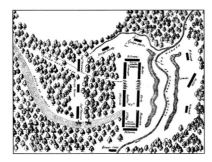

St. Clair's Battleground on the site of Fort Recovery, Ohio. (North side at bottom of cut.) Reprinted with permission of Joyce Office Products.

Even after the territory earned the right to a legislature (the Ordinance provided for this after 5000 free males had moved in), St. Clair retained extensive veto powers and was in effect a branch of the general assembly. He clearly remained the focal point of territorial power. In fact, he was very much like a colonial governor in the early days of the British Empire, a situation which made some of the settlers nervous. And since Governor St. Clair had the habit of command, a growing list of opponents over the years came to see him as overbearing and patriarchal.

Actually, he was like the fictional Marmaduke Temple and like scores of real developer-pioneers who civilized the lands from Albany to Chicago. Except for one important thing: St. Clair was not a land speculator. He had "neither the taste nor the genius for speculation in land; nor did he consider it consistent with the office." This was an unusual attitude for the times. His territorial judges and most of the Northwest's high officials were out to accumulate land. It was expected, and there was little concern for what we today call "conflict of interest."

But, like Marmaduke Temple, St. Clair was concerned primarily with *orderly settlement*, and only secondarily with freedom. There was too much freedom; St. Clair was interested in duty. Too much freedom leads to "a state of anarchy"; order was necessary to control the beast in the human heart.

Fortunately for everyone concerned, the Northwest Ordinance contained three articles which guaranteed to the citizens of the territory all the basic rights and liberties of Americans everywhere. Freedom of religion and all the other freedoms of the Common Law were spelled out in Articles I and II; Article III expressed commitment to religion, morality, and education as "necessary to good government and the happiness of mankind."

Furthermore, the law clearly required that all governments formed in the territory be *republican* governments, and that all new states should plan to "remain forever a part of this confederacy of the United States of America." In other words, the United States intended to clone themselves — their rights, laws, and governments — as the nation went west. Just to make sure that the governor and judges didn't innovate, they were limited to copying laws from the original thirteen states!

The Northwest Ordinance was the ultimate *conserving law*, except in one important respect. Article VI declared, deceptively simply: "There shall be neither slavery nor involuntary servitude in the said territory." Because this provision was added, it can be argued that the Ordinance was the best and fullest statement of American liberty written during the founding years of the republic.

The governor's job was to make this organic law work on the frontier. He and the judges and his New England-born secretary, Winthrop Sargeant, met to pass a legal code before St. Clair's first month was finished. The Code of 1788 was modified during the next three years and then fully revised in 1795. By the time the first territorial legislature met in 1798, the Old Northwest had a full framework of law and of courts. One settler said of St. Clair's arrival, "This is the birthday of the western world"; if that was true, then the laws ensured the arrival of future birthdays.

As long as the buckskin-pioneers and Indians ruled the forests, there were no laws. Frontier justice often comes with  the image of Judge Roy Bean: cigar-smokin', cussin' judges giving out hangin' sentences during the few times they can be persuaded to shut down the saloon. Or just savin' time by hangin' the varmints without botherin' folks with a trial. The image makes sense on the rugged frontier, and has been sharpened by scores of western movies. It's true that justice could be quick and rough, especially in remote areas untouched by towns. But what strikes the careful observer, and what St. Clair's career proves, is the *speed* with which the frontier was covered with the law. It was good law, too: the forms and the procedures and the substance of the English Common Law. English law was transported to America, where it took root; it was transplanted on the frontier, where it rooted again very quickly.

Reprinted with permission of Joyce Office Products.

The very first law St. Clair and his colleagues wrote created a militia. Self-defense was the great priority in Indian country. The second, third, and fourth laws created a court system: courts of Quarter-Sessions of the Peace (Justices of the Peace), Common Pleas, and Probate. These were county courts, just like back East, and St. Clair included an office of sheriff to enforce the laws. The General Court, composed of the governor and the judges, acted as a supreme court.

The whole system was English. The poet Stephen Vincent Benét once wrote,

> *And Thames and all the rivers of the kings*
> *Ran into the Mississippi and were drowned.*

But one historian has put it better: the "Thames flowed into the muddy waters of the Mississippi and transformed them, engulfed them, Anglicized them forevermore."

There were almost no volumes of American law reports, so lawyers and judges packed up William Blackstone's *Commentaries On the Laws of England* when they went west. Frontier law was continually refreshed by English books, because they were all the frontiersman had. The frontier changed Anglo-American law much less than Anglo-American law changed the frontier.

Treason headed the list of their criminal laws, because the British and the Spaniards were so close and so meddlesome. Then followed the normal list of crimes: murder, manslaughter, arson, burglary, rioting (St. Clair's concern for good order prompted them to put this high on the list), perjury, forgery, and assault. What strikes our contemporary eyes is the punishments provided: whipping (not exceeding thirty-nine stripes), forced labour for the offended person (for as long as seven years), time in stocks and pillories, fines, and death.

"Gaols" were few and inconvenient, and the theory of punishment was to punish, not incarcerate. This hadn't changed much since early colonial times.

The governor's concept of good order also extended to social and moral relations. A disobedient son or daughter could get ten stripes; public drunkenness or profane language drew fines; the Sabbath had to be observed as "greatly conducive to civilization as well as morality and piety." In the preamble to a law regulating "Gaming" (gambling), St. Clair wrote, "Whereas the population, happiness, and prosperity of all countries, especially infant communities, necessarily depend upon the sobriety and industry of the people, and their attention to the moral and political duties of life," it followed that all "gaming, sporting, or betting" ought to be strictly controlled, because they tend to "the corruption of morals and the increase of vice and idleness, and by which the honest and unsuspecting citizen may be defrauded, and deserving families be reduced to beggary and want."

Poverty was a constant problem and a threat also to good order. The longest law written by these early legislators was one for poor relief. It provided for "overseers of the poor" on the New England model, men who not only took care to see that citizens had enough to eat, but also had the authority to put children into apprenticeship programs and to find work for men and women in want.

Poverty was everywhere on the frontier. It especially affected land sales and threatened to undermine the principle of private property. Squatters without money simply took possession of the land they wanted and often defied authorities to get them off it. Abundant land was the lifeblood of the young nation, but the governor knew that land was no good unless it could be sold and worked in good order. And government was no good unless it could protect property.

St. Clair believed that land sales in the Old Northwest would not be very profitable for the national government. Rather, he said, greed for land often caused treasonous behavior; unscrupulous schemers were always hatching plots to build private empires, or detach parts of the West and join up with Spain or Great Britain. St. Clair heard reports in 1794 that the meddling French ambassador, "Citizen" Edmund Genêt, had offered French financial support for a private American army to attack Spanish New Orleans. The man he tempted with the potentially treasonous mission was none other than the great American hero of the Revolution in the west, George Rogers Clark! The very presence of great areas of unsettled land threatened to bring chaos rather than to create prosperity. Good order was the first need of all. Law was life.

In 1792 a law was passed requiring every county to build a proper courthouse and other public buildings. Local judges and officials were given control over the planning, financing, and construction. So began (or continued, from the Pennsylvania and New York frontier experiences) one of the uniquely American symbols of the presence of law in the wilderness. The typical experience was for the entire frontier community to join the project. Some people gave money. Others gave their skills as stone masons or carpenters. They loaned their oxen and horses, sent their wives and daughters to cook, and sat in endless meetings to plan the next construction steps. Very rarely did they slap together stick buildings; they built of stone and brick, on rock foundations. They put carved walnut furnishings and windows of stained glass in stately courtrooms. Their architectural models were often taken from Rome and Greece. They were, in a true sense, "Temples of the Republic."

Old court house and prison erected in Bedford in 1774. Reprinted with permission of Joyce Office Products.

Law required administration. St. Clair had the power to divide the territory into counties and townships and to appoint "such magistrates and other civil officers...as he shall find necessary for the preservation of the peace and good order in the same." Counties and towns were old English forms of local government which had been imported for colonial use. Counties had especially thrived in the southern states, and towns became characteristic of the New England region. In the Northwest Territory (and this would be the pattern for the rest of the history of the frontier) the two were combined.

Southern counties were run by the judges, and that was to be true of the Northwest Territory. Judges effectively ruled through their courtroom decisions under the Common Law. They also had a big support system. St. Clair appointed (using Virginia and Pennsylvania precedents) a sheriff, five justices of the peace, a county clerk, various officers of the militia, a coroner, assessors, and numerous officers of the court. An early sheriff wrote that "there is more law business here than might be expected by the newness of the place." The courthouse, "Law's Temple," became the center of legal activity.

Law business attracted lawyers. All over this part of the frontier lawyers would come seeking opportunity and often would act as the entrepreneurs and developer-pioneers who founded towns and built roads, canals, and, later, railroads. A young man named Lincoln went to the Illinois frontier hoping to find prosperity and political opportunity. Much of this lay in the future, but even in St. Clair's day the law business generated other business, and the fees collected by all county officials for their services made for lively and active government. That is what the governor wanted: active and energetic local officials, operating by the rules, working for progress and civil order and also getting rewarded for it.

A key local official was the justice of the peace. He had limited judicial powers, dealing mostly with property disputes among neighbors. Good justices of the peace, however, could do much for the reputation of the law. The importance of the office was acknowledged by the acute French observer of America, Alexis de Tocqueville, who described the responsibilities in the following way:

> *A justice of the peace is halfway between a man of the world and a magistrate, an administrator and a judge. A justice of the peace is an educated citizen but does not necessarily have any knowledge of the laws. For that reason his responsibility is only to be society's policeman, a matter requiring good sense and integrity more than knowledge.*

St. Clair always insisted upon appointing men of achievement and integrity to this office. As we shall see, by doing so he would help create a base of power from which opposition to him would grow, and, ironically, help to bring his own administration of the territory to an end.

New Englanders had founded the community at Marietta, and it was partly their influence that caused St. Clair gradually to pay more attention to dividing counties into townships. He started this practice in 1790, using the rules established in the Land Ordinance of 1785. That law set the essential features of frontier land policy. It provided for surveys, defined townships, set prices, and in general encouraged the orderly movement westward of an agricultural republic. A township was a block of land six miles square, further subdivided into thirty-six equal sections one mile square (640 acres), with one section set aside for the support of education.

Because Governor St. Clair gave some important functions to the township, New Englanders moving into the territory were able to make the town and the courthouse vital centers of their local political and legal life. This had been their custom and heritage. St. Clair made overseer of the poor a town office and also gave the towns control over roads, bridges, and the registration of livestock. A town clerk was to keep all records in the courthouse. These powers allowed New Englanders to bring their town meeting with them, thus guaranteeing continuity of local democracy on the frontier.

By 1795, then, just about the time the Indian threat had begun to subside, St. Clair had managed to put in place the framework of law and local government that he was convinced would hold back chaos and allow the act of creation to go forward. It wouldn't always work the way he wanted it to work.

St. Joseph County Court House, South Bend, Indiana, completed 1855. Architect John Mills Van Osdel. Photograph by Bob Thall. Reprinted with the permission of the Seagram County Court House Archives, Library of Congress.

Stark County Court House, Toulon, Illinois, c. 1857-67 with later addition. Builders Parker C. and Elias Spaulding. Photograph by Harold Allen. Reprinted with the permission of the Seagram County Court House Archives, Library of Congress.

Van Wert County Court House, Van Wert, Ohio, c. 1874-76. Architechts Thomas J. Tolan & Son. Photograph by Lewis Kostiner. Reprinted with the permission of the Seagram County Court House Archives, Library of Congress.

Montgomery County Court House, Dayton, Ohio, c. 1847-50. Architect Howard Daniels. Photograph by Allen Hess. Reprinted with the permission of the Seagram County Court House Archives, Library of Congress.

Henderson County Court House, Oquawka, Illinois, c. 1841-42. Architect unknown. Photograph by Harold Allen. Reprinted with the permission of the Seagram County Court House Archives, Library of Congress.

Ross County Court House, Chillicothe, Ohio, 1855. Architects Collins & Autenrieth. Photograph by Allen Hess. Reprinted with the permission of the Seagram County Court House Archives, Library of Congress.

Orange County Court House, Paoli, Indiana, c. 1847-50. Architect unknown. Photograph by Bob Thall. Reprinted with the permission of the Seagram County Court House Archives, Library of Congress.

Geauga County Court House, Chardon, Ohio, 1869. Architect Joseph Ireland. Photograph by Richard Pare. Reprinted with the permission of the Seagram County Court House Archives, Library of Congress.

Logan County Court House, Bellefontaine, Ohio, c. 1870-71. Architect
Alexander Koehler. Photograph by Richard Pare. Reprinted with the permission
of the Seagram County Court House Archives, Library of Congress.

Tippecanoe County Court House, Lafayette, Indiana, 1881-85. Architect Elias Max. Photograph by Bob Thall. Reprinted with the permission of the Seagram County Court House Archives, Library of Congress.

Parke County Court House, Rockville, Indiana, c. 1879-81. Architects Thomas J. Tolan & Son. Photograph by Bob Thall. Reprinted with the permission of the Seagram County Court House Archives, Library of Congress.

Switzerland County Court House, Vevay, Indiana, c. 1862-64. Architect David Duback. Photograph by Bob Thall. Reprinted with the permission of the Seagram County Court House Archives, Library of Congress.

V. "A Little Tinctured with Democracy": New England and Virginia in Ohio

Shortly after the first territorial legislature met in 1798, it was clear that Arthur St. Clair was in considerable political trouble. A "popular" party led by Nathaniel Massie, Thomas Worthington, and Dr. Edward Tiffin began to push for Ohio statehood over St. Clair's vigorous opposition, and despite the fact that the population of the territory was nowhere near the 60,000 required by the Northwest Ordinance. If one simply reads each side's propaganda, it looks like a case of aristocracy vs. democracy. St. Clair often accused his opposition of being "a little tinctured with democracy"; they in turn equated him with British-style "tyranny, unbefitting the new republic." St. Clair became a strong Federalist, the party of Washington, Hamilton, and Adams. Massie, Worthington, and Tiffin favored the Jeffersonian Democratic-Republicans.

Nathaniel Massie. Reprinted with permission of Joyce Office Products.

Actually, the conflict was not so simple as Federalist aristocracy vs. Republican democracy, although the Republican leaders wanted very much for people to read it that way. St. Clair eventually lost patience with this approach and cried, in a speech at Cincinnati, "Republicans! What is a republican? *Is there a single man in all the country that is not a republican, both in principle and in practice, except, perhaps, a few people who wish to introduce negro slavery among us?*" He was right. It was one of the many ironies of the politics of Ohio statehood that the citizens who cried "republican!" and "democracy!" loudest were those who tried several times to have the anti-slavery provision of the Northwest Ordinance overturned.

And to suppose that Massie, Worthington, and Tiffin were men of the people while St. Clair relied on government by the "rich and well-born" is simply to ignore what wealthy gentlemen the Republican leaders were! The real source of conflict was that three visions of political culture were at work in Ohio: nationalist, New England, and Southern. These political cultures were very different despite existing within the framework of a common language and broad agreement about republican forms and purposes of government.

St. Clair, let us recall, was a nationalist, and he was not an American by birth or early culture. He was raised, educated, and trained for the military as a Scot. His experience in America was in a New England family, at work on the Pennsylvania frontier, and, most important, as a general officer of the Continental Line. St. Clair was not a part of any local or regional American culture that shaped his reactions to events around him. His vision of the United States was as a *nation*, a united people committed to the orderly development of liberty and prosperity. It should also be

Old Rosslyn Castle near Edinburgh, stronghold of the St. Clair family. Reprinted with permission of Joyce Office Products.

noted that the man he admired more than anyone but George Washington was Alexander Hamilton, a fellow Scot, born in the West Indies, and himself having no loyalties to local American culture. Hamilton gained his national vision serving on Washington's general staff.

Nationalists were convinced that the great danger to the young republic was the centrifugal force of localism. Americans tended to be so jealous of their local cultures, and so tribal about their families and their churches, that the problem with America was not the danger of central power, but the good chance that the country would fly apart. From the standpoint of a St. Clair, most Americans were also undisciplined, uncouth, independent, and ignorant, as well as stubborn. When the great Methodist bishop, Francis Asbury, visited Steubenville in 1803 he said, "I feel the power of Satan in these little, wicked, western trading towns." St. Clair was the first to agree.

Second, there were the New Englanders. Winthrop Sargeant was from Massachusetts, although he was a strong nationalist and much more uncompromising than St. Clair. As Secretary of the Territory, Sargeant acted as governor when St. Clair was away on his many trips through the large Territory. The Ohio Company of Associates, which had opened Marietta, was also a company of New Englanders. The Western Reserve, a large tract up on Lake Erie that included Cleveland, was the property of Connecticut.

New England in Ohio meant towns, schools, and preachers. New Englanders preferred tight-knit little communities, towns of 1,000-3,000 people, run by town meetings. They encouraged their people to live on orderly small farms, to promote crafts and commerce, and to educate their children. All over the Northwest Territory, the enthusiasm with which transplanted New England towns built courthouses, schools, academies, and colleges is astonishing. They were Congregationalists and Presbyterians, mostly, and their preachers brought high biblical standards and stern morality to the remotest frontier. New Englanders were the supreme civilizers, and they tended to support the orderly minded Governor St. Clair.

Third, there were Southerners. Massie, Worthington, and Tiffin were Virginians who came to Ohio to establish themselves in the Virginia Military Tract. Like the Western Reserve, this was a large area set aside before the Territory was formed. It was part of a compromise whereby Virginia ceded its claims to Kentucky to the national government. The Virginians came to Ohio for the same reason most people went to the frontier: to acquire land. But they had a far different idea of what it meant to own land than either the nationalists or the New Englanders did. And therein lies the story of Arthur St. Clair's political demise.

Winthrop Sargeant, Secretary, N.W. Territory. Reprinted with permission of Joyce Office Products.

The struggle began in July, 1797, when Sargeant (acting for St. Clair) created Adams County in the Virginia Military Tract. He also appointed Nathaniel Massie and Thomas Worthington as justices of the peace, and Massie as lieutenant colonel of the militia. They were unremarkable appointments; it was St. Clair's usual practice to appoint men of local influence to such positions, and the two Virginians were among the area's largest landowners. Justices had rather large administrative powers. They could divide counties into townships, oversee poor relief and road construction, grant licenses to ferry operators, tavern owners, and merchants, appoint all local officials, and regulate taxation. Since the Virginia Military Tract had not yet been surveyed into townships, the powers of Massie, Worthington, and their friends were potentially the basis for their own "act of creation."

The controversy arose over the location of the county seat and, eventually, the courthouse. Massie wanted them near his center of speculation and land development. Despite two attempts by St. Clair to place it elsewhere, the Virginians (in 1798) took it upon themselves to hold court where they saw fit. St. Clair responded by revoking their commissions. Their actions, he said, were "contrary to every principle of good order," and "a most unwarrantable assumption of power and contempt of authority by the justices." He would not allow public authority to be dictated by what he considered motives of private gain.

The Virginians brought the matter to the first territorial legislature, held that same year, and obtained a law declaring their town the county seat. St. Clair vetoed it, insisting that such actions "introduce amongst the people a spirit of discontent, *love of innovation*, and of...intrigue, destructive of public tranquillity." To the Governor, the Virginians were promoting social anarchy for private gain. To Massie and Worthington, St. Clair was being arbitrary and tyrannical, and thwarting the will of the people. Local folks, they felt, should run their own affairs.

Thomas Worthington. Reprinted with permission of Joyce Office Products.

The political culture of the Virginians valued independence above all. While they were by no means pure buckskin-pioneers, they were men who insisted upon governing their own affairs on their own property. The ideal of the Virginia gentry, from which Massie, Worthington, and Tiffin came, was ownership of a significant amount of property worked by others. This would free them for manly outdoor activities, like hunting, horses, and politics. Slave culture was not an option in the territory (they would try unsuccessfully to change this in 1805 and 1807), but land speculation was. By accumulating massive amounts of land, the Virginians could achieve independence for their families with a minimum of physical labor and have a maximum amount of time for political leadership.

They lived by a system of personal honor, much like the code of a military officer (which St. Clair could well understand), based directly on the amount of land they owned and the degree of public leadership they could achieve. Massie, Worthington, and Tiffin were honorable men, good at land speculation, proud of their achievements, and not about to be pushed around by Arthur St. Clair. Unlike New Englanders, they had contempt for towns, preferring to build country estates on the Virginia model. Worthington had what some people considered the finest house in the West, a federal style mansion with several wings and formal gardens surrounding it.

The county court was at the center of their political culture. To be a "gentleman justice" was to control one's own destiny. To be a justice of the peace was to have one's possessions and status justified by the authority of the law. Furthermore, to be *removed* from office and accused of mere self-interestedness was a serious insult. Arthur St. Clair had made permanent enemies.

It is important to keep in mind that St. Clair was convinced that he was upholding his authority, which derived from the *nation*. He was vitally concerned with binding the West to the country as a whole, and he knew very well the spirit of anarchy which could threaten national unity. In opposing the Virginians he was trying to show that national authority took precedence over "selfishness and local spiritedness." He had written to President Washington back in 1789 that he intended to act in ways that "tend to make the Inhabitants one People." In 1800 he was still convinced that the wealthy land-owners had created a system that could be dangerous to the nation. His words are worth quoting:

> *A multitude of indigent and ignorant people are but ill-qualified to form a constitution and government for themselves; but that is not the greatest evil to be feared from it. They are too far removed from the seat of government to be much impressed with the power of the United States . . .Fixed political principles they have none, and though at present they seem attached to the General Government, it is in fact but a passing sentiment, easily changed or even removed, and certainly not strong enough to be counted upon as a principle of action.*

So the two sides locked in mortal political combat. It was honorable combat for the most part, although the advocates of early Ohio statehood could get unruly. In January of 1802, in Chillicothe, a mob fueled up by distilled spirits hanged St. Clair in effigy and invaded his hotel. St. Clair met them calmly with a brace of pistols, and they retreated. He later gave Worthington credit for having helped to disperse the more dangerous types.

St. Clair lost when the Federalists lost. Thomas Jefferson

was elected President in the "Revolution of 1800." Gradually his followers in the West gained the upper hand, and, in 1802, after a vitriolic exchange with leaders of an Ohio constitutional convention, the President fired him. St. Clair was informed by a letter from the Secretary of State, James Madison, posted not to St. Clair himself, but to one of his most bitter enemies. It was an undignified and unjustified end to a long and distinguished public career.

St. Clair Monument, Greensburg, Pennsylvania.
Reprinted with permission of Joyce Office Products.

VI. "An Act of Creation"

Not all stories end happily. Arthur St. Clair went back to western Pennsylvania and lived sixteen more years, content enough in the midst of much of his family. His personal fortunes were in shambles. He hadn't paid much attention to enriching himself during the fourteen years in the Northwest Territory, and he had taken on a great deal of administrative expense himself, always assuming the national government would pay him back. That wasn't to be. A frugal Republican administration and nasty political revenge combined to diminish his holdings further. He eventually died nearly penniless, admired by his neighbors, respected by his old friends, but forgotten by his country.

Arthur St. Clair is still ill-remembered by the nation he helped to found. The record, however, of the Northwest Ordinance and its only administrator is a crucial chapter in the book of the early republic. It perhaps fell short of being a true "act of creation." It was clearly a great *conserving* act: it established the law in the wilderness. It prompted the construction of a series of magnificent courthouses, many of which still stand as living testimony to the stabilizing influence of law and order. It kept Americans a people of the law under trying circumstances. The developer-pioneer was central to this order-keeping endeavor. Arthur St. Clair spent his life and fortune in service to the ideals of nation, order, integrity, and truth.

MINNESOTA
1858

WISCONSIN
1848

Lake Superior

MICHIGAN 1837

Lake Michigan

Lake Huron

Lake Erie

ILLINOIS
1818

INDIANA
1816

OHIO
1803

Map of the
Northwest Territory

The Northwest Territorial Government
1787

[THE CONGRESS OF THE CONFEDERATION, JULY 13, 1787.]

An Ordinance for the government of the territory of the United States northwest of the river Ohio.

Be it ordained by the United States in Congress assembled, That the said territory, for the purposes of temporary government, be one district, subject, however, to be divided into two districts, as future circumstances may, in the opinion of Congress, make it expedient.

Be it ordained by the authority aforesaid, That the estates both of resident and non-resident proprietors in the said territory, dying intestate, shall descend to, and be distributed among, their children and the descendants of a deceased child in equal parts, the descendants of a deceased child or grandchild to take the share of their deceased parent in equal parts among them; and where there shall be no children or descendants, then in equal parts to the next of kin, in equal degree; and among collaterals, the children of a deceased brother or sister of the intestate shall have, in equal parts among them, their deceased parent's share; and there shall, in no case, be a distinction between kindred of the whole and half blood; saving in all cases to the widow of the intestate, her third part of the real estate for life, and one-third part of the personal estate; and this law relative to descents and dower, shall remain in full force until altered by the legislature of the district. And until the governor and judges shall adopt laws as hereinafter mentioned, estates in the said territory may be devised or bequeathed by wills in writing, signed and sealed by him or her in whom the estate may be (being of full age) and attested by three witnesses; — and real estates may be conveyed by lease and release, or bargain and sale, signed, sealed, and delivered by the person, being of full age, in whom the estate may be, and attested to by two witnesses, provided such wills be duly proved, and such conveyances be acknowledged, or the execution thereof duly proved, and be recorded within one year after proper magistrates, courts, and registers, shall be appointed for that purpose; and personal property may be transferred by delivery, saving, however, to the French and Canadian inhabitants, and other settlers of the Kaskaskies, Saint Vincents, and the neighboring villages, who have heretofore professed themselves citizens of Virginia, their laws and customs now in force among them, relative to the descent and conveyance of property.

Be it ordained by the authority aforesaid, That there shall be appointed, from time to time, by Congress, a governor, whose commission shall continue in force for the term of three years, unless sooner revoked by Congress; he shall reside in the district, and have a freehold estate therein, in one thousand acres of land, while in the exercise of his office.

There shall be appointed from time to time, by Congress, a secretary, whose commission shall continue in force for four years, unless sooner revoked; he shall reside in the district, and have a freehold estate therein, in five hundred acres of land, while in the exercise of his office. It shall be his duty to keep and preserve the acts and laws passed by the legislature, and the public records of the district, and the proceedings of the governor in his executive department, and transmit authentic copies of such acts and proceedings every six months to the secretary of Congress. There shall also be appointed a court, to consist of three judges, and two of whom to form a court who shall have a common-law jurisdiction, and reside in the district, and have each therein a freehold estate, in five hundred acres of land, while in the exercise of their offices; and their commissions shall continue in force during good behavior.

The governor and judges, or a majority of them, shall adopt and publish in the district such laws of the original States, criminal and civil, as may be necessary, and best suited to the circumstances of the district, and report them to Congress from time to time, which laws shall be in force in the district until the organization of the general assembly therein, unless disapproved of by Congress; but afterwards the legislature shall have authority to alter them as they shall think fit.

The governor, for the time being, shall be commander-in-chief of the militia, appoint and commission all officers in the same below the rank of general officers; all general officers shall be appointed and commissioned by Congress.

Previous to the organization of the general assembly the governor shall appoint such magistrates, and other civil officers, in each county or township, as he shall find necessary for the preservation of the peace and good order in the same. After the general assembly shall be organized the powers and duties of magistrates and other civil officers shall be regulated and defined by the said assembly; but all magistrates and other civil officers, not herein otherwise directed, shall, during the continuance of this temporary government, be appointed by the governor.

For the prevention of crimes and injuries, the laws to be adopted or made shall have force in all parts of the district, and for the execution of process, criminal and civil, the governor shall make proper divisions thereof; and he shall proceed, from time to time, as circumstances may require, to lay out the parts of the district in which the Indian titles shall have been extinguished, into counties and townships, subject, however, to such alterations as may thereafter be made by the legislature.

So soon as there shall be five thousand free male inhabitants, of full age, in the district, upon giving proof thereof to the governor, they shall receive authority, with time and place, to elect representatives from their counties or townships, to represent them in the general assembly; *Provided,* That for every five hundred free male inhabitants there shall be one representative, and so on, progressively, with the number of free male inhabitants, shall the right of representation increase, until the number of representatives shall amount to twenty-five; after which the number and proportion of representatives shall be regulated by the legislature: *Provided,* That no person be eligible or qualified to act as a representative, unless he shall have been a citizen of one of the United States three years, and be a resident in the district, or unless he shall have resided in the district three years; and, in either case, shall likewise hold in his own right, in fee-simple, two hundred acres of land within the same: *Provided also,* That a free hold in fifty acres of land in the district, having been a citizen of one of the States, and being resident in the district, or the like freehold and two years' residence in the district, shall be necessary to qualify a man as an elector of a representative.

The representatives thus elected shall serve for the term of two years: and in case of the death of a representative, or removal from office, the governor shall issue a writ to the county or township, for which he was a member, to elect another in his stead, to serve for the residue of the term.

The general assembly, or legislature, shall consist of the governor, legislative council, and a house of representatives. The legislative council shall consist of five members, to continue in office five years, unless sooner removed by Congress; any three of whom to be a quorum: and the members of the council shall be nominated and appointed in the following manner, to wit: As soon as representatives shall be elected the governor shall appoint a time and place for them to meet together, and when met they shall nominate ten persons, residents in the district, and each possessed of a freehold in five hundred acres of land, and return their names to Congress, five of whom Congress shall appoint and commission to serve as aforesaid; and whenever a vacancy shall happen in the council, by death or removal from office, the house of representatives shall nominate two persons, qualified as aforesaid, for each vacancy, and return their names to Congress, one of whom Congress shall appoint and commission for the residue of the term; and every five years, four months at least before the expiration of the time of service of the members of the council, the said house shall nominate ten persons, qualified as aforesaid, and return their names to Congress, five of whom Congress shall appoint and commission to serve as members of the council five years, unless sooner removed. And the governor, legislative council, and house of representatives shall have authority to make laws in all cases for the good government of the district, not repugnant to the principles and articles in this ordinance established and declared. And all bills, having passed by a majority in the house, and by a majority in the council, shall be referred to the governor for his assent; but no bill, or legislative act whatever, shall be of any force without his assent. The governor shall have power to convene, prorogue, and dissolve the general assembly when, in his opinion, it shall be expedient.

The governor, judges, legislative council, secretary, and such other officers as Congress shall appoint in the district, shall take an oath or affirmation of fidelity, and of office; the governor before the president of Congress, and all other officers before the governor. As soon as a legislature shall be formed in the district, the council and house assembled, in one room, shall have authority, by joint ballot, to elect a delegate to Congress, who shall have a seat in Congress, with a right of debating, but not of voting, during this temporary government.

And for extending the fundamental principles of civil and religious liberty, which form the basis whereon these republics, their laws and constitutions, are erected; to fix and establish those principles as the basis of all laws, constitutions, and governments, which forever hereafter shall be formed in the said territory; to provide, also, for the establishment of States, and permanent government therein, and for their admission to a share in the Federal councils on an equal footing with the original States, at as early periods as may be consistent with the general interest:

It is hereby ordained and declared, by the authority aforesaid, that the following articles shall be considered as articles of compact, between the original States and the people and States in the said territory, and forever remain unalterable, unless by common consent, to wit:

Article I

No person, demeaning himself in a peaceable and orderly manner, shall ever be molested on account of his mode of worship, or religious sentiments, in the said territory.

Article II

The inhabitants of the said territory shall always be entitled to the benefits of the writs of *habeas corpus*, and of the trial by jury; of a proportionate representation of the people in the legislature, and of judicial proceedings according to the course of the common law. All persons shall be bailable, unless for capital offences, where the proof shall be evident, or the presumption great. All fines shall be moderate; and no cruel or unusual punishments shall be inflicted. No man shall be deprived of his liberty or property, but by the judgment of his peers, or the law of the land, and should the public exigencies make it necessary, for the common preservation, to take any person's property, or to demand his particular services, full compensation shall be made for the same. And, in the just preservation of rights and property, it is understood and declared, that no law ought ever to be made or have force in the said territory, that shall, in any manner whatever, interfere with or affect private contracts, or engagements, *bona fide*, and without fraud previously formed.

Article III

Religion, morality, and knowledge being necessary to good government and the happiness of mankind, schools and the means of education shall forever be encouraged. The utmost good faith shall always be observed towards the Indians; their lands and property shall never be taken from them without their consent; and in their property, rights and liberty they never shall be invaded or disturbed, unless in just and lawful wars authorized by Congress; but laws founded in justice and humanity shall, from time to time, be made, for preventing wrongs being done to them, and for preserving peace and friendship with them.

Article IV

The said territory, and the States which may be formed therein, shall forever remain a part of this confederacy of the United States of America, subject to the Articles of Confederation, and to such alterations therein as shall be constitutionally made; and to all the acts and ordinances of the United States in Congress assembled; conformable thereto. The inhabitants and settlers in the said territory shall be subject to pay a part of the Federal debts, contracted, or to be contracted, and a proportional part of the expenses of government to be apportioned on them by Congress, according to the same common rule and measure by which apportionments thereof shall be made on the other States; and the taxes for paying their proportion shall be laid and levied by the authority and direction of the legislatures of the district, or districts, or new States, as in the original States, within the time agreed upon by the United States in Congress assembled. The legislatures of those districts, or new States, shall never interfere with the primary disposal of the soil by the United States in Congress assembled, nor with any regulations Congress may find necessary for securing the title in such soil to the *bona fide* purchasers. No tax shall be imposed on land the property of the United States; and in no case shall non-resident proprietors be taxed higher then residents. The navigable waters leading into the Mississippi and Saint Lawrence, and the carrying places between the same, shall be common highways, and forever free, as well to the inhabitants of the said territory as to the citizens of the United States, and those of any other States that may be admitted into the confederacy, without any tax, impost, or duty therefor.

Article V

There shall be formed in the said territory not less than three nor more than five States; and the boundaries of the

States, as soon as Virginia shall alter her act of cession and consent to the same, shall become fixed and established as follows, to wit: The western State, in the said territory, shall be bounded by the Mississippi, the Ohio, and the Wabash Rivers; a direct line drawn from the Wabash and Post Vincents, due north, to the territorial line between the United States and Canada; and by the said territorial line to the Lake of the Woods and Mississippi. The middle State shall be bounded by the said direct line, the Wabash from Post Vincents to the Ohio, by the Ohio, by a direct line drawn due north from the mount of the Great Miami to the said territorial line, and by the said territorial line. The eastern State shall be bounded by the last-mentioned direct line, the Ohio, Pennsylvania, and the said territorial line: *Provided, however,* And it is further understood and declared, that the boundaries of these three States shall be subject so far to be altered, that, if Congress shall hereafter find it expedient, they shall have authority to form one or two States in that part of the said territory which lies north of an east and west line drawn through the southerly bend or extreme of Lake Michigan. And whenever any of the said States shall have sixty thousand free inhabitants therein, such State shall be admitted, by its delegates, into the Congress of the United States, on an equal footing with the original States, in all respects whatever; and shall be at liberty to form a permanent constitution and State government: *Provided,* The constitution and government, so to be formed, shall be republican, and in conformity to the principles contained in these articles, and, so far as it can be consistent with the general interest of the confederacy, such admission shall be allowed at an earlier period, and when there may be a less number of free inhabitants in the State than sixty thousand.

Article VI

There shall be neither slavery nor involuntary servitude in the said territory, otherwise than in punishment of crimes, whereof the party shall have been duly convicted: *Provided always,* That any person escaping into the same, from whom labor or service is lawfully claimed in any one of the original States, such fugitive may be lawfully reclaimed, and conveyed to the person claiming his or her labor or service as aforesaid.

Be it ordained by the authority aforesaid, That the resolutions of the 23d of April, 1784, relative to the subject of this ordinance, be, and the same are hereby, repealed, and declared null and void.

Done by the United States, in Congress assembled, the 13th day of July, in the year of our Lord one thousand seven hundred and eighty-seven, and of their sovereignty and independence the twelfth.